HEIAN ASIAN LIBRARY

中 國 歌 謠 選

FOLK RHYMES
OF
CHINA

Selected and illustrated by
Kwan Shan Mei

Translated by
Zhou Bianming

Edited by
Judy W. P. Kong

平安国际出版社
HEIAN INTERNATIONAL, INC.

© 1981, 1992 Federal Publications (S) Pte Ltd

First American Edition 1993

Heian International, Inc Publishers
P.O.Box 1013
Union City. CA 94587

ISBN 0-89346-454-6

Printed in Singapore

Geyao 歌謠 is a general name. In terms of format, this general name refers to both *ge* and *yao* which are differentiated according to their relationship with music. Verses that have been set to music are known as *ge*, which is equivalent to folk songs. Verses that are chanted unaccompanied by music are *yao*, which is equivalent to folk rhymes. In terms of content, both *ge* and *yao* give expression to man's emotions. The preface to the *Shijing (The Book of Poetry)* has this to say, 'Verses are wherein man's thoughts reside. Dwelling in man's heart, thoughts become verses when vocally expressed. Emotionally stirred, man vents his feelings in words. When words cannot express his feelings, he then sighs. When sighs cannot express his feelings, he then sings.' These lines bear testimony to the inextricable relationship between *geyao* and man's emotions.

In the history of Chinese verse, *Shijing* is the earliest collection of *geyao* consisting of works of some 500 years dating from the early Zhou Dynasty (eleventh century B.C.) to the Spring and Autumn Period (770–476 B.C.) In the Western Zhou Dynasty (1027–771 B.C.), the rulers sent officials to go to the people every year to collect, examine and record *geyao* which could enhance their knowledge of the customs and views of the people. Among the 305 pieces of the *Shijing*, apart from the song 頌 pieces which eulogize virtues and achievements and the *Daya* 大雅 pieces which describe the literati's feasts and gatherings, the *Xiaoya* 小雅 and *Guofeng* 國風 pieces are songs of the folk. Different facets of life are reflected in the *Shijing*. These include production activities such as farming, fishing and hunting, folk-ways such as weddings and funerals, the love relationship between man and woman such as courtship.

In subsequent dynasties, most of the *geyao* was committed to writing. The *geyao* of each dynasty was closely related to the social milieu of the time. Take for example, at the time of the Southern Dynasties (A.D. 420–589) which had only retained sovereignty over the southern part of the country, many new cities sprang up in southern China because people who used to live in the north flocked to the south. The Yang Prefecture and the Jing Prefecture then became the political, economic and cultural centres of the country. It was in the vicinity of these places that the *Wuge* 吳歌 (songs of the lower Yangtze) and *Xiqu* 西曲 (songs of the middle Yangtze) originated. As the traffic was busy, the trade prosperous and merchants travelled to and fro, the *Wuge* and *Xiqu* often presented glimpses of a merchant's life, for instance, scenery of the river and the wandering life of travellers. The *geyao* of this period was characterized by the depiction of love between merchants and prostitutes and the bitterness of their separation.

The folk rhymes of every dynasty are manifestations of the people's emotions. Welled up in their hearts and vocalized, the gamut of emotions finds expression in folk rhymes which are very simple, natural and unadorned. The length of the lines and the change of rhythm are modified in a very natural manner. For instance, in the verses of *Shijing*, there are usually four characters to a line, but at times there are five, six or seven. Other than the standard form which consists of four lines with five characters each, the verses of the Southern Dynasties also seek expression in other forms. For example, there can be three lines with five characters each, or there can be three characters to the first line and five characters to the last two. This shows that folk rhymes are not governed by any fixed form.

Folk rhymes are circulated and handed down by oral tradition. In the process of circulation, a folk rhyme is more often than not subjected to changes due to the differences in geographical environment, customs and dialectal variation, resulting in the enrichment of its content and the intensification of its artistic effect. Thus, a folk rhyme can have other variants.

Not only are the forms variegated, but the artistry of folk rhymes is also diversified. *Fu*賦, *Bi* 比, *Xing* 興 have since the time of the *Shijing* become the essential means of artistic expression in verses. *Fu* is description, that is, the direct narration of certain events or things. *Bi* is metaphor, that is, the comparison of the characteristics shared by the object of description and the object of comparison, so that the characteristics of the former become prominent and concrete. The composers of folk rhymes often base their metaphors on things that they know well and hence lend a note of familiarity to the metaphors. Puns, parallelisms and contrasts are commonly found techniques of comparison. Through puns, characters 字 or words 詞 that are homophonous are used to imply what the singer wants to say. As puns are usually very simple and plain, they are subtle as well as natural. Parallelisms are the enumerations of several things, one after another, for comparison. When a singer wishes to express his mingled emotions, to use just one thing for comparison is insipid. At this time, the technique of parallelism can be called into being to reinforce the tone and emphasize the intense feelings. By contrast, things that are strikingly antithetical are compared, for example, the peasants' toilsome life versus the landlords' easy life, the love of one's own mother versus the harshness of one's stepmother. This device is instrumental in reinforcing the theme of the folk rhyme. *Xing* in general is association. The sight of, for instance, plants, birds, beasts, mountains, rivers, the sun or the moon, strikes a responsive chord in one's heart and further arouses one's feelings. It is usually in the first line of a folk rhyme that this technique is adopted. Although there is sometimes no obvious link between this first line and the following lines, as these lines rhyme, the verse can still retain a sense of coherence.

Moreover, reduplications and exaggerations are extensively used. Reduplications are the repetitions of characters, for example 青青 . These newly coined bi-syllabic words are mostly adjectives which not only add a more vivid touch to the description and leave a deeper impression, but also make the lines more harmonious. By exaggeration, the singer exercises his rich imagination and overstates the characteristics of a certain person or a thing. Thus, the highly coloured image as depicted will arrest more attention.

Where the structure of folk rhymes is concerned, the device of repetition is prevalent. Folk rhymes are a kind of oral literature circulated among the folk. In order that the words can be easily remembered, the singer often chants the same thing over and over again. In many instances, a folk rhyme is divided into several stanzas whose end rhymes or metaphors may vary, but the theme, the tone and the line structure are largely the same. These artistic devices enrich the language and the lines hence become forceful, explicit and vivid. As such, folk rhymes are always very lively and rhythmic.

In terms of content, folk rhymes touch each and every aspect of life. One of the earliest kind of folk rhymes is the songs of the labourers. While they were working, be they ploughing, fishing, picking tea leaves, herding or gathering firewood, they chanted verses in accordance with the rhythm of their movements at work. These verses were often punctuated by their cries. Plaintive feelings are also registered in the lines of folk rhymes. Whenever people are discontented with their surroundings or oppressed by society, they articulate their feelings in folk rhymes. These verses are replete with the peasants' accusations against the extortion of excessive taxes, the scholars' accusations against the corrupt and incompetent government, the soldiers' accusations against conscriptions for years on end, the women's accusations against their unhappy marriages. These people may satirize or complain; in short, they just wish to release their pent-up emotions.

Other folk rhymes crystallize everyday life into language. They narrate, for instance, the momentous events of the country, the ceremonies for sacrificial offerings, the everyday trifles, the affection between lovers. Children's folk rhymes may have been improvised by children while they were playing, or composed by the children's grandmothers or mothers. They are in any case simple, interesting and portray the innocence of children.

One distinctive feature of folk rhymes is that they reflect the problems of women. Whether they live in the seclusion of their homes or toil in the field, women would chant verses to dispel their sadness whenever they meet with any mishaps. In fact, folk rhymes are fraught with the problems of women. That is why they are reckoned as the literature of women. This collection aptly lends support to this view as many folk rhymes here expose the misery of oppressed women. In the traditional Chinese society, men were regarded as superior to women. In the olden days, women since their birth were looked down upon by their parents.. They were whipped, scolded, sold or given away. If their parents had died early, they would have to depend on their brothers and sisters-in-law for their livelihood, meanwhile tasting the bitterness of living under other people's roof. After getting married, they would have to slave away, waiting upon their in-laws, and most of them could not escape the fate of being maltreated by the latter. If there was mutual understanding between them and their husbands, life would be easier. Nevertheless, marriages arranged by the parents and matchmakers were rarely satisfactory.

Instances of unhappy marriages existed in plenty, for example, the wife might be older than the husband; a beautiful maid might be married to an ugly or bedridden man; a husband who would not engage himself in any occupation, but instead indulge in gambling and lingering in the brothels, neglecting his obligations to the family. As relationships with members of the husbands' families were rarely harmonious and conjugal life was unhappy, these women often thought of their parents and looked forward to pouring out their woes and grievances in the presence of their parents. Yet when they returned to their parents' homes, they might be cold-shouldered by their brothers and sisters-in-law. Many of them would then place their hopes on their sons but when their sons grew up, got married, and established their careers, there was every likelihood that they would forget about the love of their mothers. What the folk rhymes record are not fictional tales, but a chorus of heart-wrenching complaints founded on actual occurrences and honest feelings. They are indeed the life history of women of the old society. Other folk rhymes in this collection depict the passion of lovers, the artlessness of children, and ceremonies and customs observed during the New Year or a wedding.

In literary history, folk rhymes have always been dismissed as popular literature of the unlettered populace. They are regarded as unworthy of any literary merit. But undoubtedly, these verses voice the aspirations of the people and reflect their daily life. To understand the thoughts and feelings of the people of a nation, and the politics and institutions of a particular era, folk rhymes are indeed the best source.

This collection endeavours to introduce to readers the customs and conditions of old China. However, various difficulties are encountered in translating these Chinese folk rhymes into English. Since folk rhymes have a close relationship with language itself, many salient features inherent in the Chinese language cannot be retained in the translation. Within these lines,

横也絲來竪也絲
The warp, the woof — they are all silk.

(See page 27)

奴空想隔年桃核舊時仁
I think in vain of the meat of the peach-stone left from yesteryear.

(See page 153)

In these lines, 絲 and 仁 are puns respectively. 絲 is a pun on another Chinese character 思 meaning 'lovesickness'. Thus 絲 in this context not only refers to the silk that is used to weave a handkerchief, but also implies lovesickness. 仁 is a pun on 人 meaning 'man'. Hence 仁 refers to the meat of the peach-stone and at the same time alludes to the former lover. In the English language, it is difficult to find such equivalents. And in the translated text, the literal meanings of these Chinese characters have been kept, with the implied meanings given in the footnotes.

The following lines present another type of translation difficulty.

山上青青是嫩葉
Green, green, tender leaves on the hill.

水底青青是嫩苔
Green, green, tender mosses at the water's bed.

(See page 11)

In this example, 青青 is a reduplication. To show that a reduplication is used as an adjective in the original, the adjective of the translated line can under certain circumstances be reiterated, as in the first quoted example. However, this translation technique cannot be used indiscriminately.

Another problem is the translation of the Chinese lines that rhyme, for example,

鬼貴陽，鬼貴陽
Cuckoo! Cuckoo!

有錢莫討後來娘
Don't take a stepmother even if there is the money.

(See page 167)

Here, the technique of *Xing* is employed in the first line which describes the cries of a bird. The only obvious link between this line and the following is that they rhyme. Yet to translate the lines in such a way that they also rhyme is not at all easy. As a result, the sense of coherence present in the original verse may not be conveyed.

Though difficulties abound in translating these folk rhymes, this is still a meaningful task for it helps to paint a picture of the Chinese folkways for western readers. Nevertheless, up till now, Chinese folk rhymes have rarely been translated into foreign languages. The publication of this collection is indeed an attempt to arouse the interest of other people in the translations of Chinese folk rhymes.

Judy W. P. Kong

一年去，一年來，
又見梅花帶雪開。
梅花落地成雪片，
開窗等雪望郎來。

Year in and year out,
Plum blossoms flower again in the snow.
Fallen petals become snowflakes on the
    ground.
I open the window, await the snow and my
    lover.

石榴花開葉兒青，
做雙花鞋望母親；
母親耽我十個月，
哪個月裏不擔心。

Green are the leaves of pomegranates that
    blossom.
Sewing a pair of embroidered shoes, I look
    at mother
Who carried me for ten months in her
    womb.
Was there a month when she was not
    worried?

手拿一張無情狀，

急急忙忙，跑入公堂。

告俺的爹娘，愛銀錢，將奴賣在烟花巷。

到烟花，今日姓李，明日姓張，

夜夜換新郎。

到晚來，思想起來恨斷腸。

久以後，奴的結果在誰身上？

Holding a plaint concerning a heartless
   cause,
I run to the law court in haste
To sue my father and mother
Who for money
Have sold me to a brothel.
At the brothel,
Dame Li I'd be this day,
Dame Zhang I'd be the morrow.
Each night there'd be a change of groom.
At dusk, heart-rending my hatred is,
As I think to whom in the end I shall
   belong.

欲寫情書，我可不識字。
煩個人兒，使不得！
無奈何，
畫幾個圈兒爲表記。
此封書惟有情人知此意：
單圈是奴家，雙圈是你。
訴不盡的苦，一溜圈兒圈下去。

I want to write a love-letter,
But I'm illiterate.
Shall I trouble someone to do it?
But that would be inappropriate.
No way out, what to do?
I draw circles as my code.
Only my lover can understand what this
    letter means.
One circle is me,
Two circles are you.
Endless lovesickness to tell,
Endless circles to be drawn.

山上青青是嫩葉，
水底青青是嫩苔。
面前有個嬌娥妹，
寬行兩步等兄來。

Green, green, tender leaves on the hill.
Green, green, tender mosses at the water's
   bed.
Lovely and fair is the lass right ahead.
'Slacken thy pace and wait for thy dearie.'

麻野鵲，尾巴長，
娶了媳婦忘了娘。
把娘背在山後頭，
把媳婦抱在炕頭上。
作盤菜，作碗湯。
媳婦媳婦你先嘗。

Long is the tail of the wild sparrow.
Having got a wife, he forgets his mother.
Back on the hill he leaves his mother.
Onto the kang* he carries his wife.
Be it a dish of fare,
Be it a bowl of soup.
'My dear wife, do taste it first.'

* kang: heatable brick platform for sleeping

姐兒長到十七八，暗暗背地怨爹媽，
別樣事兒都會辦，單把奴家留在家。
咬銀牙，淚如麻，
活活把人暗氣殺，
哎，活活把人暗氣殺。

Seventeen going on eighteen,
The lass in secret blames her parents.
'They can get all sorts of things done,
But me they choose to leave me at home.
I gnash my teeth,
I shed my tears.
They have really irritated me unto death.
O, they have really irritated me unto
    death.'

相思牌兒在門前掛，
買相思來，來問咱。
借問聲：　"這相思你要多少價？"
　"這相思得來的價兒大。"
買得搖頭，賣得把嘴咂：
　"請回來！　奉讓一半與尊駕。"

Hanging on the door is the sign 'Love-for-
   Sale'.
Here comes a lover
Who asks me,
'May I ask,
How much is this love of yours worth?'
'To get this love, the price is high.'
The inquirer shakes his head.
Pursing my lips, I say,
'Please come back.
For your honour's sake, half the price
   will do.'

寶塔高，掛鐮刀。
鐮刀快，割韭菜。
韭菜長，割兩行。
韭菜短，割兩碗，
公一碗，婆一碗。
打去了一個榴花碗，
公又鞭，婆又鞭，
嚇得小媳婦溜上天。

High is the pagoda,
A sickle is hitched.
Sharp is the sickle,
Leeks are cut.
For leeks that are long,
Two rows are cut.
For leeks that are short,
Two bowls are cut.
One bowl is for father-in-law,
One bowl is for mother-in-law.
O, she breaks a pomegranate bowl.
Father-in-law whips her,
Mother-in-law whips her.
So frightened is she that she hurries away.

昨夜晚，記得清，
明明記得郎訪情。
明明與郎說了話，
明明與郎換了心，
夢中思想一個人。

Last night it was,
I do remember clearly.
Clearly I remember, my lover had called.
Clearly I talked to you, my dearest dear.
Clearly we made a solemn pledge of love.
Only, my lover appeared in my dream.

隔花陰，遠遠望見個人來到。
穿的衣，行的步，
委實苗條，與冤家模樣兒生得一般俏。
巴不能到跟前，忙使衫袖兒招。
粉臉兒還紅，羞也!
姐姐，你把人兒認錯了!

Through clusters of flowers,
I see someone approaching from afar.
Judging from his attire,
Judging from his gait,
He is really lean
And as handsome as my beloved.
Too anxious to have him come near,
I wave my hand at him,
My powdered face still blushing, being
    shy.
'O lady,
You have mistaken me for your man.'

妹下河邊洗手巾，
低頭低腦不如人，
旁人問妹是怎樣？
妹夫年老妹年輕。

I do the washing down at the river,
Drooping my head as if I were inferior.
A looker-on asks me, 'What's the matter?'
'Old is my husband, but young am I.'

不寫情詞不寫詩，
一方素帕寄心知。
心知接了顛倒看，
橫也絲來竪也絲*，
這般心事有誰知？

*絲即思，雙關語。

Neither love-letters nor poems do I write,
To my loved one I would send a kerchief
    plain and white.
He would look at it this way and that.
The warp, the woof — they are all silk.
Who knows such thoughts of mine?

* The Chinese character for 'silk' is 絲 which is a pun on
  another character 思 meaning 'lovesickness'.

一進門兒喜冲冲，
院子裏頭搭大棚，
洞房屋裏把燈點，新媳婦一旁淚盈盈。
新郎不住的來回觀，
說："你不吃點東西兒，我可心疼。"

Right inside the gate, how merry it is!
In the courtyard, a big awning has been
    raised.
In the nuptial chamber, lamps are lit.
The bride aside is in tears.
The groom keeps pacing to and fro,
And says, 'Do eat something,
Or my heart will ache.'

娘罵女兒小賤貨，
生活勿做聽山歌；
山歌郎嘴裏嘸好歌，
唱你轉去做老婆。
女兒叫聲勿要罵我，
你年輕頭裏也愛聽山歌。
你勿聽山歌哪有我，
我勿聽山歌哪有外孫叫舅婆。

Mother scolds her daughter for being a
    contemptible wretch,
Who listens to rustic songs, neglecting her
    work.
'No good songs come from him the singer
Who sings to make you his wife.'
The daughter replies, 'Don't scold me!
You were fond for rustic songs when you
    were young.
If you hadn't listened to rustic songs,
How could I have been born?
If I didn't listen to rustic songs,
Whence would come a grandchild to call
    you grandma?'

獨自一個添愁悵，忽聽門外一派聲響。

慌的奴步出香閨，把門開放，

無有人。教奴不知怎麼樣？

哎！心哪！你再也別把他想。

說不想，由不得。

倚定門兒將他望，

等他來，和他算個清白賬。

Being alone adds to my melancholy.
Bang! Suddenly there is a noise outside.
So frightened am I that I walk out of my
    boudoir,
And open the door.
Nobody is there.
What am I to do?
O, my heart!
Think of him no more.
I tell myself not to think,
But I can't help thinking.
I lean on the door and wait for him.
Wait till he comes,
I'll settle my account with him.

石上洗衫劉三妹，借問阿哥哪裏來?
自古山歌從口*出，
哪有山歌船載來!

* "從口"與"松口"雙關。"松口"是
客家山歌著名的地方，在梅縣。

Washing on the rock, the third daughter of
the Liu family
Asks, 'Young man, where do you come
from?
From of old, rustic songs have been
delivered by the mouth.
When have such songs been carried by
boat?'

* The Chinese characters for 'have been delivered by the
mouth' are 從口. This is a pun on the name of a place Mei
County 梅縣, Songkou 松口 which is famous for Hakka
music songs.

天上的星顆顆黃。地上的小姑無爺娘。

有爺有娘金活寶，無爺無娘一根草。

堂前梳頭哥哥罵，厨房洗臉嫂子嫌。

　"哥哥你莫罵，嫂子嫂子你莫嫌，

在屋裏過不到三五年。"

In the sky, golden is each and every star.
On earth, neither father nor mother has
　　this maid.
With a father or a mother, she'd be as
　　precious as gold.
Without a father or a mother, she's but a
　　blade of grass.
Elder brother scolds her when she combs
　　her hair in the front hall.
Sister-in-law censures her when she
　　washes her face in the kitchen.
'Brother, don't scold me,
Sister-in-law, don't censure me.
I won't be staying in this house for more
　　than three years.'

姐兒肚痛呷薑湯，
半夜裏私房養個小孩郎。
玉指尖尖抱在紅燈下看，
半像奴奴半像郎。

Suffering from bellyache, the lass sips
　　ginger broth.
At midnight in her room she gives birth to
　　a baby boy.
She holds the baby in her arms under the
　　candle.
'Half the baby resembles me, and half
　　resembles him.'

紅豆獨生一個子，
好叫相思不用多。
燈蕊用來織細布，
真心不怕別人唆。

The love pea breeds only one seed,
Nor does love have to be prolific.
A wick can be used for weaving fine cloth.
A true heart fears no abettor.

大河裏洗菜，菜葉兒漂，

見一遭來想一遭。

人多眼雜難開口，石上栽花兒不牢靠。

肉兒小嬌嬌！生生教你想壞了，

呀！生生教你想壞了。

She washes vegetables by the river.

The leaves drift on the water.

Every time I see her, I'll think of her
  afterwards.

With so many people around, it's difficult
  to say anything.

Planting flowers on a rock, they can hardly
  be firm.

O my bonnie love, my sweet!

How I have been thinking of you!

O, how I have been thinking of you!

44

敢唱山歌敢大聲，
敢放白鴿敢響鈴。
燈草拿來搭橋過，
有心相愛敢同行。

I dare sing rustic songs, I dare sing out
    loud.
I dare let loose the pigeon, I dare sound
    the bell.
Rushes are used to build a bridge.
Truly loving each other, we dare walk
    together.

烟鍋不通想個法，
用根紅草通順它。
拾柴姑娘長得好，
唱個山歌逗引她。

The pipe bowl is blocked.
What's to be done?
Clear it with the wick grass.
Fair is the damsel picking firewood.
Let me sing a rustic song to tease her.

娘女倆結識一個郎，
今朝郎來哪人當？
清水裏紅菱嫩格甜，
彎角烏菱老格香。

Both the madam and her girl have known
    this man.
Who is to meet him when he comes
    today?
In clear water, the red water-chestnut is
    tender and sweet,
The black crescent-shaped water-chestnut
    is old and fragrant.

50

鏡子兒，你忒煞情淺。
我愛你清光滿，體態兒圓。
那一日不與你相親面？
我悶你也悶，我歡你也歡。
轉眼見他人也，你又是一樣臉。

O looking-glass!
You are really void of sentiments.
I love your clear full brightness,
Your full round shape.
Is there a day when I don't see you face to
    face?
When I'm sad, you're sad.
When I'm glad, you're glad.
But once you turn to some one else,
You show a different face.

村中狗咬鬧柔柔，
情哥流落在外頭，
我要開門又怕娘罵我，
只說花鞋忘記在門口。

Bow wow! The dogs are barking in the
    village.
For my lover is loitering outside.
I'd like to open the door,
But I'm afraid mother will scold me.
I will just say, 'I've left my shoes outside.'

黃狗，黃狗，你看家，
我在園中採紅花。
一朵紅花採不了，雙雙媒人到我家。
"我家女兒年紀小，不會服侍大人家！"

Yellow doggie, yellow doggie,
You look after the house.
I'm going to pick red flowers in the
    garden.
I haven't even picked one red flower,
When matchmakers in pairs come to our
    house.
'Our girl is still too young.
She knows not how to wait upon the
    grown-ups.'

弗見子情人心裏酸，
用心摸擬一般般。
閉子眼睛望空親個嘴，
接連叫句俏心肝。

Not seeing my loved one, I'm much
    grieved.
I imagine that I am seeing him.
I close my eyes, throw a kiss in the air,
And call out, 'My dear, my darling dear.'

十八女兒九歲郎，
晚上抱郎上牙牀。
"不是公婆雙雙在，
你做兒來我做娘！"

The lass is eighteen, her husband only
    nine.
Every night she has to take him up to bed.
'Weren't it that my in-laws are both alive,
You could be my son and I your mama.'

好六叔，好六舅，
借我六斗六升好綠豆。
到了秋，收了豆，
再還六叔六舅六斗六升好綠豆。

My good sixth paternal uncle,
My good sixth maternal uncle,
Lend me six pecks and six pints of good
    green grams.
When autumn comes,
And grams are cropped,
I'll duly return to sixth uncles, paternal
    and maternal,
Six pecks and six pints of good green
    grams.

荷葉上的水珠兒轉，
姐兒一見用綫穿，
怎能够一顆一顆穿成串？
不成望水珠兒大改變，
這邊散了那邊去團圓。
閃煞了奴，偏偏都被風吹散。
後悔遲，見面不如不見面!

On the lotus leaf, pearls of water are
　　rolling
The moment she sees them, she tries to
　　thread them together,
How can she pierce them one after
　　another into a string?
Hopeless! The watery pearls transform
　　themselves.
Having fallen apart on this side, they
　　reunite on the other.
'How they have deserted me!
The wind just blows them apart.
Too late for remorse!
To have seen them is worse than not
　　having seen them.'

罰了願再不把相思害，
猛可的撞見個俊多才，
不由人見了心中愛。
正是拆了秦樓瓦，又蓋上楚陽台；
賣了相思，又把相思買。

I have vowed never again to suffer from
    lovesickness.
Suddenly I come across one who is
    handsome and talented.
I just can't help loving him from the
    bottom of my heart.
O, really, after the Qin Tower* has been
    pulled down,
The Chu Terrace* is then built.
Having disposed of one love,
I acquire another.

---

* In Chinese, the phrase 'the Qin Tower and the Chu House'
  秦樓楚館 refers to brothels.

擔水便擔上步水，
莫擔下步水有砂。
連情便連大屋妹，
連人親婦是殘花。

Fetch water from the upper stream,
Fetch not from the lower stream where
    there is sand.
Select your love from girls of big families,
For in picking another man's wife you get
    only a withered flower.

打破花碗砌條街,
砌條花街等哥來。
十年不來十年等,
再不移花別等栽。

I smash a flowered bowl to pave a street.
I pave a flowered street to wait for my
lover.
Though he may not turn up after ten
years,
I'll still wait for him.
Never will I plant the flowers elsewhere.

當初甘願來交情，
兩人講過千年情。
兩人好比河中水，
河中無水正斷情。

At that time we were willing to make a
    solemn pledge of love.
We two spoke of love of a thousand years.
We two are like water in the river.
When there is no more water in the river
Our love will come to an end.

花喜鵲，站樹梢，
張三娶了個女姣姣。
擔擔水，擰擰腰，
可把張三疼極了。

On the tip of the tree
Perches the magpie.
Zhang San is married to a bonnie lass.
Carrying water, she walks swayingly.
This makes Zhang San feel very uneasy.

清晨起，冷呵呵，挽起袖子就刷鍋。

大鍋刷個明净細，小鍋刷過賽堂鑼。

叫聲小姑子凑把火，我到上房問公婆。

頭一句没作聲，再一句生氣了：

"今天有我你問我，明天無我你靠何？"

鼓靠鼓，鑼靠鑼，

新娶媳婦靠公婆，二龍取水靠天河。

Getting up early in the morning,
I find the weather very cold.
Rolling up my sleeves, I begin scouring
    pots and pans.
Cauldrons are scoured spotlessly clean.
Pots are scoured bright as gongs.
There is a call, 'Little daughter, make the
    fire.'
I go upstairs to ask my in-laws about that.
To the first question, there is no reply.
To the second question, they become
    irritated.
'Today when I'm alive, you can ask me.
On the morrow when I'm no more, on
    whom can you depend?'
The drum depends on the drum,
The gong depends on the gong,
The new bride depends on the in-laws,
The water gods, for water, depend on the
    Milky Way.

鑼鼓喧天，不覺又是一年，
新門神就把舊門神掀。
舊門神道：我在前，五顏六色曾當過道。
到如今，風吹日曬，把顏色改變。
我的哥，我的哥，
我只看你金盔金甲熬不過半年。

The deafening sounds of gongs and drums
    leap to the sky.
Another year has passed before one
    realizes it.
The new door-god replaces the old one.
The old door-god says,
'Previously, bright with many colours,
I have held sway.
But now having been blown by the wind
And exposed to the sun,
These colours have all changed.
O brother of mine,
O brother of mine,
I bet that your golden helmet and armour
    cannot last for half a year.'

冤家進門你別睡，街坊家出了個匪類。

走過來走過去，說奴生的肥。

我是一個婦人家，怎肯出去與他對？

等他來時你去把他推。

你去外面推。奴在窗戶洞裏幫着你啐！

My dear husband, don't go to bed once
　you come home.
There's a hooligan roaming in our
　neighbourhood.
Loitering here and there,
He says that I am the fat sort.
I am a woman.
How can I go out to confront him?
When he comes, you go and drive him
　away.
While you go to drive him away,
I'll spit at him from the window!

郎在山上唱高腔，
姐在河裏洗衣裳。
郎唱山歌望望姐，
姐捶三下望望郎，
小大姐下下捶在石板上。

The lad sings out loud on the hill.
The lass washes clothes by the river.
Singing rustic songs, the lad glances at the
    lass.
After pounding every three strokes, the
    lass glances at the lad,
Pounding each and every time on the
    stone.

石板搭橋千年生，
叮囑貴妹長長行，
燈草掛在蕉樹尾，
莫聽人言斷哥情。

Built of stone, the bridge is good for a
　　thousand years.
You can always walk on it, my sweetheart.
The rush is hung on the banana tree.
Don't listen to others and sever the ties of
　　our love.

新年來到，糖糕祭竈。
姑娘要花，小子要炮；
老頭子要戴呢帽，
老婆要吃大花糕。

New Year is here.
Sweets and cakes are offered to the
    kitchen god.
Young lasses want to have flowers.
Small boys want to have firecrackers.
Old men want to put on woollen caps.
Old women want to eat large fancy cakes.

脚聲兒，必定是冤家來到。
挽破了紙窗兒，偷着眼把他瞧。
悄悄的站了多時，怎不開言叫？
露濕衣衫冷，渾身似水澆，
多心的人兒也，凍的真個好。

The patter of footsteps –
My loved one must have arrived.
I tear a hole in the lattice window,
And steal a look at him.
Silently he stands there for a long time.
Why doesn't he say a word?
His clothes wet from the dew,
He is chilled as if drenched through.
He who is so furtive
Really deserves to be frozen stiff.

傻俊角，我的哥!
和塊黄泥兒捏咱兩個。
捏一個兒你，捏一個兒我;
捏的來一似活托，捏的來同牀上歇臥。
將泥人兒摔碎，着水兒重和過，
再捏一個我。
哥哥身上也有妹妹，
妹妹身上也有哥哥。

You handsome fool,
My darling dear,
Let me knead this yellow clay into you and
   me,
Knead one that is like you,
Knead one that is like me,
As if they were really you and me,
So that they may lie and rest on the bed.
Smash now these clay figures to pieces,
Mix them with water again,
Then knead another me.
In your clay figure there is me,
In my clay figure there is you.

一見情人朝後退，十指尖尖用手兒推:
"爲甚麼皮着個臉蛋，在我的跟前跪?
在何大吃得這等醺醺醉?
花街柳巷任意施爲。
從今後，不許你上我的牀來睡!
就是上牀來，也是各人蓋各人的被! "

On seeing my lover I draw back,
Pushing him away with my slender fingers.
'What brazen impudence!
Why kneel in front of me?
Where did you get so drunk?
Must be doing what you like at those
    brothels!
Hereafter I'll not allow you to sleep on my
    bed.
Even if you got on my bed,
You'd keep your own quilt and I'd keep
    mine.'

門前一株棗，
歲歲不知老。
阿婆不嫁女，
那得孫兒抱?

The date tree in front of the house.
Gets older year after year without realizing
　　it.
If mother does not marry off her daughter,
How can she have a grandchild to carry?

送情人一送在房門外，千叮萬囑咐：
　"你早早回來！家中又没有人兒在。
我身又有病，肚裏又懷胎，
我愛吃一個酸梅，哥！有錢無人買。"

Seeing my lover off at the door of the
　　room,
I remind him over and over again,
'Do come back early.
There's no one at home.
I'm ill and expecting.
I'd love to eat a pickled plum, my dear,
But there's no one to buy it for me though
　　I've the money.'

96

早朝行過妹門頭，
見娘照鏡正梳頭。
怎得兄成洗面布，
共娘相識掛心頭。

Passing by her house early in the morning,
I see her combing her hair by the looking-
    glass.
How could I become her towel,
Get acquainted with her and be together
    with her?

初更鼓，叫句天。

天啊！做甚生奴該下賤，

奴身不幸爲女子，更嫁夫，不得人。

兩脚半屎臭泥氣，情性凶惡猛虎形。

嫖賭飲吹件件有，學偷懶，學沙塵。

化我妝奩還未了，連典家財有餘剩。

柴草家財有餘剩，柴草有條米有升。

若勸半句佢嘸合，拳脚交加立到身。

When the first watch of the night is struck,
I cry out to Heaven,
Good Heavens!
Why do I have to lead such a degrading life?
Unluckily born to be a girl,
I'm married to one who is so incompetent.
How his dirty feet stink!
He is as fierce as a tiger!
He sows wild oats, gambles, drinks and
    smokes opium.
He is lazy,
And inflated with arrogance.
Having spent my dowry,
He now pawns what remains of our property.
What remains of our property is the firewood –
A piece of firewood and a sheng* of rice.
Any word of advice is disagreeable to him,
And he'll immediately give me a good cuff
    and kick.

* sheng: a unit of dry measure for grain, equivalent to one litre

蛤蟆青蛙叫連天，
想討老婆又無錢。
拿張凳子同爺講，
阿爺搖頭又一年。

The frog croaks up to the skies.
He wants to get married, but has no
    money.
Sitting on a stool, he speaks to father,
Who shakes his head and postpones it for
    another year.

小花雞，上磨盤，
娘打孩子不紡綿。
　"娘，你慢打，你慢罵，
還能在家過幾年？"
過今天，過明年，
花轎抬到大門前。
爺頓脚，娘拍手，
再有閨女搬給狗。

A little chick climbs up the milestone.
Mother whips the girl for not spinning
　　cotton.
'Mother, don't whip me,
Don't scold me.
How many more years would I stay at
　　home?'
Today passes, another year will go,
When the bridal chair is brought before
　　the house.
Father stamps his feet,
Mother claps her hands,
'Should we have another girl, we'd give
　　her to the dog.'

做天難做四月天，
蠶要温和麥要寒。
種菜哥哥要天雨，
採桑娘子要晴乾。

To be the weather of the fourth month is
   difficult.
The silkworms want it to be temperate,
The wheat wants it to be cold.
Growing vegetables, the lad wants it to be
   rainy.
Plucking mulberry leaves, the lass wants it
   to be fine.

天上星多月弗多，
和尚在門前唱山歌。
道人問道：　"師父那了能快活？"
"我受子頭髮討家婆。"

Stars there're many in the sky, but not the
　　moon.
The monk sings rustic songs in front of
　　the house.
The Taoist priest asks,
'What's the matter, master?
Why are you so gay?'
'I'm growing my hair to get married.'

高高山上一枝槐，
手爬槐樹望郎來。
娘問女兒：“望甚麼？”
“我望槐花幾時開。”

Holding on to the locust tree on the high
　　hill,
She looks for her lover's arrival.
Mother asks the daughter,
'What're you looking at?'
'I'm trying to find out when the locust will
　　blossom.'

新打鐮刀不用磨，
有情不用話頭多。
三對五句成雙對，
如同月亮照山河。

A newly-forged sickle need not be
    sharpened
Nor are many words needed when there is
    love.
Three or five words suffice to
    communicate the sentiments,
Like the moon shining upon hills and
    rivers.

養活猪吃口肉，
養活狗會看家，
養活猫會拿耗子，
養活你這丫頭作甚麼？

A pig is reared for the pork.
A dog is kept to look after the house.
A cat is kept to catch mice.
What is the use of bringing up a girl like
    you?

鴉雀喳喳，哭回娘家。

爹爹不在家，告訴給我媽：

"媽呀媽，你的女兒命不好。

嫁個丈夫不成材，

又吃鴉片烟，又打十字牌。

三天不買米，四天不買柴。

這個日子叫你心肝女兒怎樣過得來？"

'Caw! Caw!' cries the crow,
As I go weeping to my parents' home.
Father is not at home.
I'll talk to mother.
'O mother, mother dear,
Your daughter is ill-fated,
Now that she is married to an incompetent
    husband.
He smokes opium,
He gambles on dominoes,
For three days he hasn't bought any rice,
For four days he hasn't bought any
    firewood.
How can your dear daughter live like this?'

有個大姐正十七，
過了四年二十一；
尋個丈夫才十歲，
她比丈夫大十一。
一天井台去打水，
一頭高來一頭低；
不看公婆待我好，
把你推到井裏去。

There was this lass who was seventeen.
Four years later as she becomes twenty-
    one,
A ten-year-old husband is found for her.
She is eleven years older than he.
One day as they carry a bucket to draw
    water from the well,
She is at the higher end of the pole and he
    at the lower.
'If my in-laws had not treated me well,
I would have pushed you into the well.'

我的兒，我的姣。
三年不見，長得這麼高。
　"騎着我的馬，拿着我的刀：
扛着我的案板，賣切糕 。"

My little wee boy,
My darling beauty!
For three years I haven't seen you,
And you've grown so tall.
'Ride now this horse of mine,
Take now this knife of mine,
Shoulder now this chopping board of
　　mine,
As I go to sell slices of cakes.'

姐見子郎來哭起來，
那能你多時弗走子來？
來弗來時回絕子我，
省得我南窗夜夜開。

Seeing her loved one she begins to weep.
'Why haven't you been here for so long?
You should have told me whether you
    were coming or not,
So that I need not open the southern
    window night after night.'

一把扇子兩面綠，
親姐過路不進屋。
還是哪回待錯你，
不是殺鷄就稱肉。

Green is the fan on both sides.
Our sister does not enter our house when
    she passes by.
'When, indeed, have we offended you?
Have we not always treated you with
    chicken or meat?'

我們情義重過山，
海裏水深挑不乾，
烏雲做傘遮得遠，
月亮做燈照得寬。

Weightier than the mountain, our love is
As inexhaustible as the water of a deep
    sea.
Sheltering far and near, the black clouds –
    our umbrella.
Shining far and wide, the moon – our
    lamp.

小公鷄，挑草多。

俺娘給我説老婆，

説個老婆鍋台高，

正間燒火不見了。

東也找，西也找，

老鼠窩兒找到了。

The little rooster plays with the grass.
Mama has found a wife for me.
My wife is as tall as the kitchen sink.
While I'm making fire, she disappears.
I search for her hither,
I search for her thither,
At last I find her in the rat hole.

眼淚汪汪哭向郎，
我吃腹中有孕要人當。
娑婆樹底下乘涼奴踏月，
水漲船高難隱藏。

My eyes brimming with tears, I tell my
   lover,
'For that which is in my womb,
Someone must be responsible.'
Strolling in the shade of the dancing trees
   below the moon,
I feel that the tide has risen,
The boat has floated up,
And nothing more can be hidden.

郎要丟情姐不丟，
二人江邊看水流。
江心一雙鴛鴦鳥，
飛來飛去落沙洲，
只許交情不許丟。

He wishes to break off the relationship,
   but she wishes not.
They watch the flowing water by the river.
'Look at the pair of mandarin ducks in the
   midst of the river.
They fly back and forth, alighting on the
   sandbank.
Do keep up the relationship, don't break it
   off.'

132

柏公樹柴不好燒，
無夫妹子不好嫖。
有日貪花受到孕，
天井撐船難開篙。

The cypress wood is not a good fuel.
An unmarried maid is not good to flirt
    with.
If you covet her beauty and she becomes
    expectant,
You'll find it difficult to pole a boat in a
    courtyard.

當初遠見遠搖手。
如今遠見遠低頭。
哥有哪門得罪妹，
冷冷落落把哥丟。

Formerly you waved your hand seeing me
    from afar.
Now you lower your head instead.
When on earth have I offended you,
    sweetheart?
What has made you leave me out in the
    cold?

今日走過妹門邊，
不見姣妹好心焦。
心想進門看看妹，
旁人冷眼利如刀。

Today I passed by my love's house.
Not seeing my love, I became anxious.
I wanted to go in to see her,
But sharp as knives are other people's
    critical eyes.

青石頭，響叮噹，
我爹賣我不商量。
賣的銀錢還了帳，
不與小奴做陪房。

Dingdong, jingle pieces of rocks.
Without consulting me, father has sold me.
The money he's got is used to pay his
    debts,
And not given to me as my dowry.

送情人，直送到花園後，
禁不住淚汪汪滴下眼梢頭。
長途全靠神多佑，
逢橋須下馬，
有路莫登舟。
夜晚的孤單也，
少要飲些酒。

I see my lover off.
All the way to the back of the garden,
And cannot help tears welling up in my
 eyes.
'May the gods bless you in your long
 journey.
Dismount from your horse when you cross
 a bridge.
Don't travel by boat when there's a road.
When you feel lonely at night,
Don't drink too much wine.'

捎書人，出得門兒驟。
趲丫環喚轉來，
我少吩咐了話頭。
你見他時，
切莫說我因他瘦。
現今他不好，
說與他又添憂；
若問起我身軀也，
只說災晦從没有。

The courier darted out of the house.
I send the maid to call him back.
'I haven't told you what to say.
When you see him,
Don't say that I've grown thin because of
     him.
Now that he's not so well himself.
To tell him that would only add to his
     worries.
If he asks about my health,
Just say that I've had no trouble at all.'

我勸情人醒醒吧，
醒來之時吃杯香茶。
吃罷茶，趁着月色回家吧。
不回家，太爺太太心中掛。
就是你那令正夫人，也盼你回家。
回家去，千萬別説咱倆相好的話；
説出來，你受嘟囔我挨罵。

I say to my lover, 'Do wake up!
Wake up and drink a cup of fragrant tea.
After you've drunk the tea,
Hurry back home while there's still
    moonlight.
If you don't go back,
Your parents will be worried.
Even your wedded wife
Is also expecting you home.
When you go home,
Pray don't tell them about our
    relationship.
If you do,
They'll mutter against you and scold me.'

妹相思，
不作風流到幾時?
只看風吹花落地，
不見風吹花上枝。

Lovesick am I.
If I don't fall in love now, when will I?
Look, the wind blows and flowers fall on
    the ground.
Never does one see the wind blow them
    up the branches.

148

哥哥唱歌不思量，
句句唱在妹身上。
若有別人聽見了，
妹妹面皮放那當。

When you sing, my dear, you are really
	inconsiderate,
For every word you sing is about me.
If you are heard by someone else
Where, o where can I hide my face?

150

天上星多月弗明，
池裏魚多水弗清。
朝裏官多亂子法，
阿姐郎多亂子心。

When there are many stars in the sky,
The moon is not bright.
When there are many fishes in the pond,
The water is not clear.
When there are many officials at court,
The law is ill-administered.
When there are many suitors,
The maid is confused.

畫里看人假當真，
攀桃接李强爲親。
郎做了三月楊花隨處滾，
奴空想隔年桃核舊時仁*。

*仁即人，雙關語。

The man in the painting is taken for the
real.
To graft the peach on the plum, they are
forced to wed.
Having become the poplar of the third
month, he drifts about.
I think in vain of the meat of the peach-
stone left from yesteryear.

* The Chinese character for 'meat is 仁 which is a pun on
another character 人 , meaning 'man'.

小板凳，歪一歪，
聽見樓上媳婦哭下來。
公公婆婆問甚事？
她說：	"丈夫不存財，
三天不買米，四天不買柴，
問問這個日子怎樣過得來？"

The wooden stool totters.
The weeping daughter-in-law is heard
	coming downstairs.
The in-laws ask, 'What's the matter?'
She says, 'My husband hasn't left any
	money with me.
For three days we haven't bought any
	firewood.
May I ask, how can we live like this?'

思想妹，
蝴蝶思想也爲花。
蝴蝶思花不思草，
兄思情妹不思家。

I think of my love.
The butterfly thinks of the flower.
The butterfly thinks of the flower, not the
  grass.
I think of my dear love, not my home.

曾送你玉簪兒，載也不載？

曾送你青絲帶，可曾繫來？

曾送你汗巾兒，在也不在？

曾送你一把銷金扇，

曾送你一隻半新不舊的紅睡鞋，

這幾件要緊東西也，

如何問着佯不睬？

I've sent you a jade hatpin.
Why haven't you worn it?
I've sent you a blue silk sash.
Have you ever worn it?
I've sent you a cummerbund.
Do you still have it?
I've sent you a golden-rimmed fan.
I've sent you a red slipper which is no
    longer new.
When I ask you about these few important
    things,
Why do you pretend not to have heard
    me?

神前下，十八家，
朝朝起來望水花。
無米煮，煮泥沙；
無床睡，青天下；
無被蓋，竹葉遮。

At Shenqian*,
There are eighteen families.
Every morning the people rise to look at
the splashes of water.
Having no rice,
They cook mud and sand.
Having no bed,
They sleep under the blue sky.
Having no quilt,
They cover themselves with bamboo
leaves.

* Shenqian is a dangerous shoal at the Weng River 翁江
whose source is in Wengyuan 翁源 in the Guangdong
Province 廣東省.

小小鷄，遍身黃，
那個女兒不想娘？
想來想去無處去，
關起門來哭一場。
雖說公婆待我好，
那及自己老子娘？

The little chick is yellow all over.
Is there any daughter who does not think
    of her mother?
However I may long for her, there is
    nowhere else to go.
I close the door and have a good cry.
Though my in-laws treat me well,
How can they be compared to my dear
    mother?

俏哥哥，我吩咐你再不要吃醉。

今日裏，緣何吃得醉如泥?

陪你的，想是個青樓妓。

我且饒了你，也要自三思:

　"她若果有你的真心也，

怎捨得醉了你? "

My darling dear,
I tell you, don't ever get drunk again.
Why are you today as drunk as a lord?
She who kept you company,
Must be a whore.
I'd forgive you this time,
But you also have to think it over.
If she really loved you,
Would she allow you to become so drunk?

鬼鬼楊，鬼鬼楊，
有錢莫討後來娘。
前娘殺雞留雞腿，
後娘殺雞留雞腸。
雞腸掛在楊樹上，
想起前娘哭一場。

Cuckoo! Cuckoo!
Don't take a stepmother even if there is
    the money.
When my own mother kills a chicken,
She leaves the drumstick for me.
When my stepmother kills a chicken,
She leaves the intestines for me.
Hanging the intestines on the poplar,
And thinking of my own mother,
I burst into tears.

挑水妹，
打爛水桶不敢回：
一來又怕家婆罵，
二來又怕老公搥。

She who fetches water
Has broken the bucket and dare not go
    home.
Firstly, she is afraid that her mother-in-law
    will scold her.
Secondly, she is afraid that her husband
    will whip her.

我這心裏一大塊，
左推右推推不開。
叫丫環，請個大夫與我理理脈。
那大夫一進門連聲咳:
　"也不是病來也不是災，
這就是情人留下的相思債。"

There is in my heart this big lump
Which can neither be pushed to the left
　　nor to the right.
I told my maid
To send for the doctor to feel my pulse.
On entering the house, the doctor sighs
　　again and again,
'Neither illness nor disaster is this,
It's just the lover's debt left behind to be
　　paid.'

小寡婦兒身穿孝，
手拿着紙錢到荒郊。
上新墳口口聲聲把兒夫叫：
撇下你父母年老，兒女幼小，
我上無倚來下無靠。
若死了！ 你在陰司怎知道？
你在陰司怎知道？

In deep mourning the widow
Goes to the wilderness with offerings.
At the new grave, she wails and weeps for
    her deceased husband.
'You've deserted your aged parents,
You've deserted your young children.
There're no older ones in the family whom
    I can rely on,
There're no younger ones whom I can
    depend on.
But you're dead!
How could you know this in the
    netherworld?
How, indeed, could you know this in the
    netherworld?'

"爲甚麼不點燈？"
"外面刮大風。"
"爲甚麼不關門？"
"外面還有人。"
"爲甚麼不梳頭？"
"無有桂花油。"
"爲甚麼不洗臉？"
"無有胰子鹼。"
"爲甚麼不帶花？"
"丈夫不在家。"

'Why isn't the lamp lit?'
'Because a gale is blowing outside.'
'Why isn't the door closed?'
'Because there're still people outside.'
'Why don't you comb your hair?'
'Because there's no cassia oil.'
'Why don't you wash your face?'
'Because there's no soap.'
'Why don't you wear flowers?'
'Because my husband's not at home.'

蒲欏車，大馬拉，
嘩啦嘩啦到娘家。
爹出來，抱包袱；
娘出來，抱娃娃；
哥出來，抱匣子；
嫂子出來，一扭撻。
　"嫂子嫂子你別扭，
當天來，當天走，
不吃你飯，不喝你酒。"

Click-a-clack!
Drawn by high horses
The rush cart arrives at my parents'
　home.
Father comes out
To take the bundle.
Mother comes out
To carry the baby.
Elder brother comes out
To take the casket.
Sister-in-law comes out
Walking swayingly.
'Sister-in-law, don't walk so.
We come today,
And leave today.
Neither would we eat your rice,
Nor drink your wine.'

日頭當頂又打斜，
十八大姐在送茶，
擦得汗來太陽曬。
打得傘來汗又淌，
不是情深誰送茶。

The sun has been overhead and is veering
    to the west.
The eighteen-year-old lass delivers tea.
While she is wiping the sweat away,
She is exposed to the sun.
While she is unfurling the parasol,
Sweat drips again.
Had it not been for deep love,
Who would bother about delivering tea?